INTRODUCTION

Welcome to the **Healthy Smoothie Recipe Book: The Ultimate Guide to Quick, Easy, and Nutrient-Packed Blends for Detox, Weight Loss, and Energy-Boosting**. This book is your comprehensive guide to creating nutritious and delicious smoothies that will help you achieve your health and wellness goals.

Smoothies are an excellent way to incorporate a wide range of nutrients into your diet in a convenient and tasty manner. Whether you're looking to lose weight, boost your energy levels, or simply enjoy a refreshing and healthy treat, this book has something for everyone:

- **Boost Your Nutrient Intake:** Smoothies are packed with vitamins, minerals, antioxidants, and fiber, which are essential for maintaining good health.
- **Aid in Weight Loss:** With the right ingredients, smoothies can help you feel full and satisfied, reducing the temptation to snack on unhealthy foods.
- **Increase Energy Levels:** Smoothies made with energy-boosting ingredients like fruits, vegetables, and protein can provide a quick and sustained energy boost.
- **Promote Overall Wellness:** Regularly consuming smoothies can support a healthy immune system, improve digestion, and enhance overall well-being.

TABLE OF CONTENTS

CHAPTER 1:
SMOOTHIE ESSENTIALS

Smoothies are a quick and convenient way to enjoy a nutritious meal or snack. Understanding the basics can help you create a balanced and delicious smoothie every time.

ESSENTIAL INGREDIENTS FOR DELICIOUS AND HEALTHY SMOOTHIES

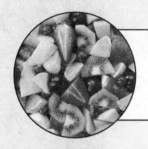

01 FRUITS
Fresh or frozen fruits like bananas, berries, mangoes, apples, and pineapples add natural sweetness and a variety of nutrients.

02 VEGETABLES
Leafy greens like spinach and kale, as well as other veggies like carrots, cucumbers, and beets, boost the nutritional value of your smoothie

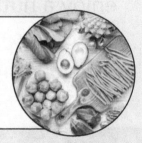

03 LIQUIDS
Water, dairy milk, almond milk, coconut water, and fruit juices are popular bases that help achieve the desired consistency.

04 PROTEIN SOURCES
Greek yogurt, protein powders, nut butters, and seeds like chia or flax add protein and make your smoothie more filling.

05 HEALTHY FATS
Avocados, nuts, seeds, and coconut oil provide essential fats that help keep you satisfied

06 NATURAL SWEETENERS
Honey, maple syrup, or agave nectar can enhance the flavor without relying on refined sugars.

TOOLS AND EQUIPMENT

Creating the perfect smoothie requires some basic tools and equipment

01 BLENDER

A high-powered blender ensures a smooth and creamy consistency, but a standard blender can also work with a bit more effort.

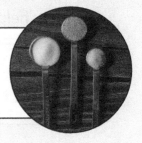

02 MEASURING CUPS AND SPOONS

Accurate measurements help maintain consistency in flavor and texture.

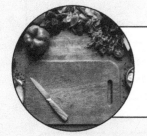

03 KNIFE AND CUTTING BOARD

For prepping fresh fruits and vegetables.

04 STORAGE CONTAINERS

Mason jars or reusable containers for storing smoothies or prepped ingredients.

05 STRAWS AND LIDS

Eco-friendly options like stainless steel or bamboo straws for convenient sipping.

BLENDING TECHNIQUES FOR PERFECT SMOOTHIES

1 **LAYERING INGREDIENTS**

Start with liquids at the bottom, followed by soft ingredients (like yogurt or bananas), and then add frozen fruits and ice on top. This helps prevent the blender from getting stuck.

2 **BLEND IN STAGES**

Blend greens and liquids first until smooth, then add fruits and other ingredients. This ensures a smoother texture.

3 **PULSE AND STIR**

If using a regular blender, pulse the ingredients and stir occasionally to ensure everything blends evenly.

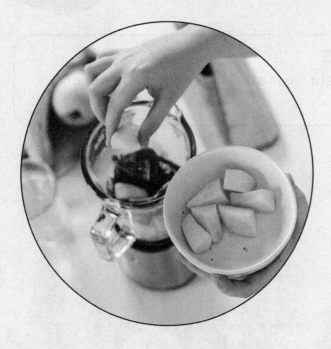

HOW TO CHOOSE THE BEST FRUITS AND VEGETABLES

SEASONAL PRODUCE

Opt for in-season fruits and vegetables for the best flavor and nutrition.

ORGANIC OPTIONS

Whenever possible, choose organic produce to reduce exposure to pesticides.

RIPENESS

Use ripe fruits for natural sweetness and better blending. Overripe fruits can also be great for smoothies.

STORING AND PRESERVING INGREDIENTS

01 FREEZING
Freeze fresh fruits and vegetables in pre-portioned bags to save time and reduce waste. Blanch leafy greens before freezing to preserve nutrients.

02 REFRIGERATION
Store fresh produce in the refrigerator to maintain freshness. Use airtight containers to keep prepped ingredients from spoiling.

03 SHELF-STABLE ADDITIONS
Keep pantry items like protein powders, seeds, nuts, and sweeteners in a cool, dry place.

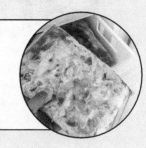

04 PRE-MADE SMOOTHIE PACKS
Combine all your smoothie ingredients (except liquids) in freezer bags. When ready to blend, just add your liquid base and blend.

By understanding these smoothie essentials, you'll be well-equipped to create delicious, nutritious smoothies that fit your lifestyle.

HAPPY BLENDING!

CHAPTER 2: DETOX SMOOTHIES

Detox smoothies are a delicious and effective way to cleanse your body, boost your energy levels, and improve your overall health. By incorporating nutrient-rich ingredients, these smoothies help eliminate toxins, promote digestion, and support your body's natural detoxification processes.

BENEFITS OF DETOXIFYING YOUR BODY

1 **Removes Toxins**

Detox smoothies aid in flushing out harmful toxins that accumulate in the body from environmental pollutants, processed foods, and other sources. Ingredients like leafy greens, lemon, and ginger help stimulate the liver and kidneys, enhancing their ability to detoxify your system.

2 **Boosts Energy Levels**

The nutrient-dense ingredients in detox smoothies provide your body with essential vitamins and minerals, leading to increased energy and vitality. Natural sugars from fruits combined with fiber and healthy fats offer sustained energy without the crash associated with refined sugars.

3 **Improves Digestion**

Many detox smoothies include ingredients that promote healthy digestion, such as fiber-rich fruits and vegetables, ginger, and probiotics like yogurt. These components help maintain a healthy gut, reduce bloating, and improve regularity.

4 **Supports Weight Loss**

Detox smoothies are often low in calories but high in essential nutrients, making them a great addition to a weight loss regimen. They can help control cravings, reduce appetite, and provide a healthy alternative to high-calorie snacks and meals.

5 **Enhances Skin Health**

The vitamins and antioxidants found in detox smoothies, such as vitamin C from citrus fruits and beta-carotene from carrots, contribute to healthy, glowing skin. Detoxifying the body can also reduce acne and other skin issues caused by toxins.

6 **Strengthens the Immune System**

Ingredients like berries, leafy greens, and citrus fruits are packed with immune-boosting nutrients like vitamin C, antioxidants, and phytochemicals. Regular consumption of detox smoothies can help bolster your body's defenses against illnesses.

7 **Promotes Mental Clarity**

By eliminating toxins and providing a steady supply of essential nutrients, detox smoothies can enhance brain function and mental clarity. The antioxidants and omega-3 fatty acids found in certain smoothie ingredients support cognitive health and reduce inflammation.

Green Detox Delight Smoothie

Ingredients

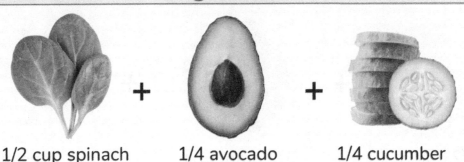

1/2 cup spinach + 1/4 avocado + 1/4 cucumber

1 tspn fresh ginger + 1/4 lemon, juiced + 1/4 green apple + 1 tspn chia seeds

+ 1/2 cup coconut water or water (and ice for a thicker smoothie)

Directions

- **Prepare Ingredients**
  - Wash the spinach and cucumber thoroughly.
  - Peel and chop the cucumber and avocado.
  - Core and chop the green apple.
  - Juice the lemon.
  - Peel and grate the ginger.

- **Blend Ingredients**
  - In a blender combine the spinach, cucumber, avocado, green apple, lemon juice, grated ginger, chia seeds, and the coconut water.
  - Blend until smooth.
  - Taste and add optional honey or maple syrup if needed. Blend until well combined.

- **Serving Suggestions**
  - Garnish with a slice of lemon or cucumber for an added touch.
  - Sprinkle additional chia seeds or flax seeds on top for extra fiber and texture.

Citrus Cleanse Smoothie

Ingredients

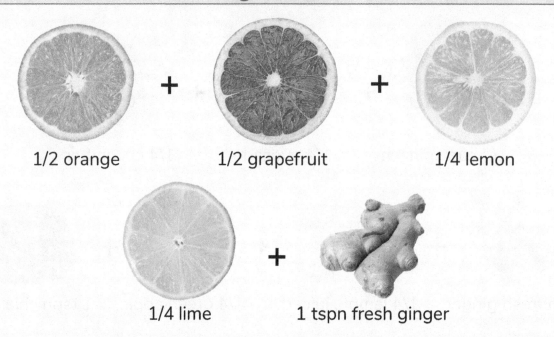

1/2 orange + 1/2 grapefruit + 1/4 lemon

1/4 lime + 1 tspn fresh ginger

+ 1/2 cup coconut water or water (and ice for a thicker smoothie)

Directions

- **Prepare Ingredients**
  - Peel and segment the orange and grapefruit.
  - Juice the lemon and lime.
  - Peel and grate the ginger.

- **Blend Ingredients**
  - In a blender combine the orange and grapefruit segments, lemon and lime juice, grated ginger, and the coconut water or water.
  - Blend until smooth.
  - Taste and add optional honey or maple syrup if needed. Blend until well combined.

- **Serving Suggestions**
  - Garnish with a slice of orange or grapefruit for an extra citrusy touch.
  - Sprinkle additional chia seeds or flax seeds on top for added fiber and texture.

Calories: 120 kcal. Protein: 2g. Carbohydrates: 30g. Fat: 1g. Fiber: 5g

Berry Boost Detox Smoothie

1/2 cup mixed berries + 1/4 banana + 1/4 cup spinach

1 tspn fresh lemon juice + 1 tspn chia seeds

+ 1/2 cup almond milk or water (and ice for a thicker smoothie)

Directions

- **Prepare Ingredients**
  - Wash the berries and spinach.
  - Peel the banana and break it into chunks.

- **Blend Ingredients**
  - Add the almond milk or water to a blender.
  - Add the mixed berries, banana, spinach, lemon juice, and chia seeds.
  - Blend until smooth.
  - Taste and add optional honey or maple syrup if needed. Blend until well combined.

- **Serving Suggestions**
  - Top with a few whole berries or a sprinkle of chia seeds for a decorative touch.
  - Add a dollop of Greek yogurt for extra creaminess and protein.

Tropical Detox Elixir Smoothie

Ingredients

1/2 cup pineapple chunks + 1/4 banana + 1/4 cup mango chunks + 1/4 cup spinach

1 tspn fresh lime juice + 1 tspn fresh ginger + 1 tspn chia seeds

+ 1/2 cup coconut water or water (and ice for a thicker smoothie)

Directions

- **Prepare Ingredients**
  - Peel and chop the pineapple, mango, and banana.
  - Wash the spinach.
  - Peel and grate the ginger.

- **Blend Ingredients**
  - Add the coconut water or water to a blender.
  - Add the pineapple chunks, mango chunks, banana, spinach, lime juice, grated ginger, and chia seeds.
  - Blend until smooth.
  - Taste and add optional honey or maple syrup if needed. Blend until well combined.

- **Serving Suggestions**
  - Garnish with a slice of lime or a wedge of pineapple for an extra tropical touch.
  - Sprinkle additional chia seeds or flax seeds on top for added texture and nutrition.

Calories: 180 kcal. Protein: 3g. Carbohydrates: 40g. Fat: 2g. Fiber: 8g

Beetroot Bliss Smoothie

Ingredients

1/4 cup blueberries + 1/2 cup strawberries + 1/4 banana

1/4 cup Greek yogurt or a dairy-free alternative + 1/2 small beetroot + 1 tspn chia seeds

+ 1/2 cup almond milk or water (and ice for a thicker smoothie)

Directions

- **Prepare Ingredients**
  - Peel and chop the beetroot.
  - Hull the strawberries.
  - Peel the banana and break it into chunks.

- **Blend Ingredients**
  - Add the coconut water or water to a blender.
  - Add the chopped beetroot, strawberries, blueberries, banana, Greek yogurt, and chia seeds.
  - Blend until smooth.
  - Taste and add optional honey or maple syrup if needed. Blend until well combined.

- **Serving Suggestions**
  - Garnish with a sprinkle of chia seeds or a few whole berries for a decorative touch.
  - Serve with a slice of whole grain toast or a handful of nuts for added protein and fiber.

Lemon Ginger Detox Smoothie

Ingredients

1/2 lemon

\+

1 tspn fresh ginger

\+

1 tspn honey or maple syrup

1/4 tspn turmeric powder

\+

1/4 tspn cinnamon

\+

1/4 cup Greek yogurt or a dairy-free alternative

\+ 1/2 cup water or coconut water (and ice for a thicker smoothie)

Directions

- **Prepare Ingredients**
  - Peel and seed the lemon.
  - Peel and grate the ginger.

- **Blend Ingredients**
  - Add the coconut water or water to a blender.
  - Add the peeled and seeded lemon, grated ginger, honey or maple syrup, turmeric powder, cinnamon, Greek yogurt.
  - Blend until smooth.

- **Serving Suggestions**
  - Garnish with a slice of lemon or a sprinkle of cinnamon for an extra burst of flavor.
  - Serve with a small handful of nuts or seeds for added protein and crunch.

Calories: 80 kcal. Protein: 4g. Carbohydrates: 15g. Fat: 1g. Fiber: 3g

Apple Cucumber Refresher Smoothie

Ingredients

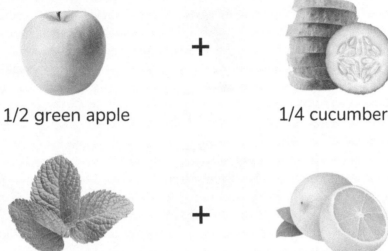

1/2 green apple + 1/4 cucumber

3-5 fresh mint leaves + 1/4 lemon

+ 1/2 cup coconut water or water (and ice for a thicker smoothie)

Directions

- **Prepare Ingredients**
  - Core and chop the green apple.
  - Peel and chop the cucumber.
  - Juice the lemon.

- **Blend Ingredients**
  - Add the coconut water or water to a blender.
  - Add the chopped green apple, chopped cucumber, lemon juice, and fresh mint leaves.
  - Taste and add optional honey or maple syrup if needed. Blend until well combined.

- **Serving Suggestions**
  - Garnish with a sprig of fresh mint or a slice of cucumber for an extra refreshing touch.

Spinach Mint Detox Smoothie

Ingredients

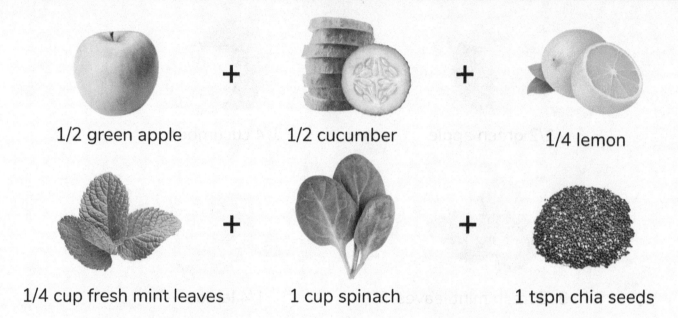

1/2 green apple + 1/2 cucumber + 1/4 lemon

1/4 cup fresh mint leaves + 1 cup spinach + 1 tspn chia seeds

+ 1/2 cup coconut water or water (and ice for a thicker smoothie)

Directions

- **Prepare Ingredients**
  - Wash the spinach and mint leaves.
  - Peel and chop the cucumber.
  - Core and chop the green apple.
  - Juice the lemon.

- **Blend Ingredients**
  - Add the coconut water or water to a blender.
  - Add the spinach, mint leaves, chopped cucumber, chopped green apple, chia seeds and lemon juice.
  - Taste and add optional honey or maple syrup if needed. Blend until well combined.

- **Serving Suggestions**
  - Garnish with a sprig of fresh mint or a slice of cucumber for an elegant presentation.
  - Serve with a side of a handful of almonds for added protein and texture.

Calories: 100 kcal. Protein: 2g. Carbohydrates: 25g. Fat: 1g. Fiber: 5g

Pineapple Parsley Cleanse Smoothie

Ingredients

 +

1 cup fresh pineapple chunks   1/2 cucumber

 +

1/4 cup fresh parsley leaves   1/4 lemon

+ 1/2 cup coconut water or water (and ice for a thicker smoothie)

Directions

- **Prepare Ingredients**
  - Cut the fresh pineapple into chunks.
  - Wash the parsley leaves.
  - Peel and chop the cucumber.
  - Juice the lemon.

- **Blend Ingredients**
  - In a blender combine the coconut water or water, fresh pineapple chunks, parsley leaves, chopped cucumber, and lemon juice.
  - Blend until smooth.
  - Taste and add optional honey or maple syrup if needed. Blend until well combined.

- **Serving Suggestions**
  - Garnish with a sprig of fresh mint or a slice of cucumber for an elegant presentation.
  - Serve with a side of a handful of almonds for added protein and texture.

Carrot Ginger Cleanser Smoothie

Ingredients

1 large carrot + 1 tspn fresh ginger

1/2 apple + 1/4 lemon

+ 1/2 cup water or coconut water (and ice for a thicker smoothie)

Directions

- **Prepare Ingredients**
  - Peel and chop the carrots.
  - Peel and grate the ginger.
  - Core and chop the apple.
  - Juice the lemon.

- **Blend Ingredients**
  - Add the coconut water or water to a blender.
  - Add the chopped carrots, grated ginger, chopped apple, and lemon juice.
  - Blend until smooth.
  - Taste and add optional honey or maple syrup if needed. Blend until well combined.

- **Serving Suggestions**
  - Garnish with a slice of apple or a sprinkle of cinnamon for an extra flavor boost.

Calories: 120 kcal. Protein: 2g. Carbohydrates: 30g. Fat: 1g. Fiber: 5g

Watermelon Mint Detox Smoothie

Ingredients

1 cup cubed watermelon

8-10 fresh mint leaves

1/4 cucumber

1/4 lime

+ 1/2 cup water or coconut water (and ice for a thicker smoothie)

Directions

- **Prepare Ingredients**
  - Cube the watermelon, removing any seeds.
  - Wash the mint leaves.
  - Peel and chop the cucumber.
  - Juice the lime.

- **Blend Ingredients**
  - In a blender combine the coconut water or water, cubed watermelon, mint leaves, chopped cucumber, and lime juice.
  - Add optional honey or agave syrup if needed.
  - Blend until smooth.

- **Serving Suggestions**
  - Garnish with a sprig of mint or a slice of watermelon for a fresh and vibrant presentation.

Celery Green Detox Smoothie

Ingredients

2 celery stalks	1/2 green apple	1/4 cucumber
3-5 fresh parsley leaves	1/4 lemon	3-5 fresh mint leaves

+ 1/2 cup water or coconut water (and ice for a thicker smoothie)

Directions

- **Prepare Ingredients**
  - Chop the celery stalks.
  - Core and chop the green apple.
  - Peel and chop the cucumber.
  - Juice the lemon.
  - Wash the parsley and mint leaves.

- **Blend Ingredients**
  - In a blender combine the coconut water or water, chopped celery, chopped green apple, chopped cucumber, lemon juice, parsley leaves, and mint leaves.
  - Blend until smooth.
  - Taste and add optional honey or maple syrup if needed. Blend until well combined.

- **Serving Suggestions**
  - Garnish with a sprig of parsley or a slice of cucumber for an added touch of freshness.
  - Serve with a side of whole grain toast or a handful of nuts for a balanced snack.

Calories: 70 kcal. Protein: 1g. Carbohydrates: 15g. Fat: 0.5g. Fiber: 4g

Kiwi Kale Cleanse Smoothie

Ingredients

1/2 green apple + 1 cup kale leaves

1 kiwi + 1/4 lemon

+ 1/2 cup water or coconut water (and ice for a thicker smoothie)

Directions

- **Prepare Ingredients**
  - Peel and chop the kiwis.
  - Remove the stems from the kale leaves and chop them.
  - Core and chop the green apple.
  - Juice the lemon.

- **Blend Ingredients**
  - In a blender combine the coconut water or water, chopped kiwis, chopped kale leaves, chopped green apple, and lemon juice.
  - Add optional honey or agave syrup if needed.
  - Blend until smooth.

- **Serving Suggestions**
  - Garnish with a slice of kiwi or a sprinkle of chia seeds for a decorative touch.

Blueberry Basil Detox Smoothie

Ingredients

1/2 cup blueberries
(fresh or frozen)

+

8-10 fresh basil leaves

1/4 lemon

+

1/4 cucumber

+ 1/2 cup water or coconut water (and ice for a thicker smoothie)

Directions

- **Prepare Ingredients**
  - If using fresh blueberries, wash them.
  - Wash the basil leaves.
  - Peel and chop the cucumber.
  - Juice the lemon.

- **Blend Ingredients**
  - Add the coconut water or water to a blender.
  - Add the blueberries, basil leaves, chopped cucumber, and lemon juice.
  - Add optional honey or agave syrup if needed.
  - Blend until smooth.

- **Serving Suggestions**
  - Garnish with a sprig of basil or a few extra blueberries for a pop of color.
  - Serve with a side of Greek yogurt or a sprinkle of granola for added protein and texture.

Calories: 80 kcal. Protein: 1g. Carbohydrates: 20g. Fat: 0.5g. Fiber: 3g

Grapefruit Green Detox Smoothie

Ingredients

 +  +

1/2 grapefruit   1 cup spinach leaves   5-8 fresh mint leaves

 +  +

1/2 green apple   1/4 cucumber   1/4 lemon

+ 1/2 cup water or coconut water (and ice for a thicker smoothie)

Directions

- **Prepare Ingredients**
  - Peel and segment the grapefruit.
  - Wash the spinach leaves and mint leaves.
  - Core and chop the green apple.
  - Peel and chop the cucumber.
  - Juice the lemon.

- **Blend Ingredients**
  - In a blender combine the coconut water or water, grapefruit segments, spinach leaves, chopped green apple, chopped cucumber, mint leaves, and lemon juice.
  - Add optional honey or agave syrup if needed.
  - Blend until smooth.

- **Serving Suggestions**
  - Garnish with a slice of grapefruit or a sprig of mint for a fresh and vibrant presentation.

Turmeric Tonic Smoothie

Ingredients

1/2 banana + 1/2 orange + 1/4 cup pineapple chunks (fresh or frozen)

1/4 tspn ground turmeric + 1/4 tspn fresh ginger + 1 tspn fresh lemon juice

+ 1/2 cup water or coconut water (and ice for a thicker smoothie)

Directions

- **Prepare Ingredients**
  - Peel and chop the banana.
  - Peel and segment the orange.
  - Peel and chop the ginger.

- **Blend Ingredients**
  - Add the coconut water or water to a blender.
  - Add the banana, orange segments, pineapple chunks, ground turmeric or fresh turmeric, ground ginger or fresh ginger, and lemon juice.
  - Add optional honey or agave syrup if needed.
  - Blend until smooth.

- **Serving Suggestions**
  - Garnish with a slice of orange or a sprinkle of turmeric powder for a vibrant touch.
  - Add a pinch of black pepper to enhance the absorption of turmeric.

Calories: 110 kcal. Protein: 1.5g. Carbohydrates: 27g. Fat: 0.5g. Fiber: 3g

Coconut Lime Cleanser Smoothie

Ingredients

 +  +

1/2 cup coconut milk   1/2 banana   1/4 avocado

 +  +

1/4 lime   1 tspn shredded coconut (optional, for extra coconut flavor)   1 tspn coconut oil

+ 1/4 cup coconut water (and ice for a thicker smoothie)

Directions

- **Prepare Ingredients**
  - Peel and chop the banana.
  - Peel and pit the avocado.
  - Juice the lime.

- **Blend Ingredients**
  - In a blender, combine the coconut milk, coconut water, coconut oil, chopped banana, avocado, and lime juice.
  - Add the shredded coconut if using and blend until smooth.
  - Taste and add optional honey or maple syrup if needed. Blend until well combined.

- **Serving Suggestions**
  - Garnish with a lime wedge or a sprinkle of shredded coconut for a tropical touch.

Raspberry Lemon Detox Smoothie

Ingredients

 +

1/2 cup raspberries
(fresh or frozen)

1/2 banana

 +

1/4 lemon

1/4 cucumber

+ 1/2 cup water or coconut water (and ice for a thicker smoothie)

Directions

- **Prepare Ingredients**
  - Peel and chop the banana.
  - Peel and chop the cucumber.
  - Juice the lemon.

- **Blend Ingredients**
  - Add the coconut water or water to a blender.
  - Add the raspberries, chopped banana, chopped cucumber, the lemon juice.
  - Add optional honey or agave syrup if needed.
  - Blend until smooth.

- **Serving Suggestions**
  - Garnish with a few whole raspberries or a slice of lemon for a vibrant presentation.
  - Serve with a side of Greek yogurt or a sprinkle of granola for added protein and texture.

Calories: 90 kcal. Protein: 1.5g. Carbohydrates: 23g. Fat: 0.5g. Fiber: 6g

Avocado Detox Dream Smoothie

Ingredients

1/2 avocado + 1/2 banana + 1/4 cucumber

1/2 cup spinach leaves + 1/2 lime

+ 1/2 cup water or coconut water (and ice for a thicker smoothie)

Directions

- **Prepare Ingredients**
  - Peel and pit the avocado.
  - Peel and chop the banana.
  - Wash the spinach leaves.
  - Peel and chop the cucumber.
  - Juice the lime.

- **Blend Ingredients**
  - Add the coconut water or water to a blender.
  - Add the avocado, chopped banana, spinach leaves, chopped cucumber, and lime juice.
  - Add optional honey or agave syrup if needed.
  - Blend until smooth.

- **Serving Suggestions**
  - Garnish with a slice of lime or a few spinach leaves for a fresh presentation.

Strawberry Detox Splash Smoothie

Ingredients

 + 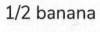 +

| 1/2 cup strawberries (fresh or frozen) | 1/2 banana | 1/4 cup pineapple chunks (fresh or frozen) |

1/4 cucumber + 1/2 lemon

+ 1 cup water or coconut water (and ice for a thicker smoothie)

Directions

- **Prepare Ingredients**
  - Hull and chop the strawberries if fresh.
  - Peel and chop the banana.
  - Peel and chop the cucumber.
  - Juice the lemon.

- **Blend Ingredients**
  - Add the coconut water or water to a blender.
  - Add the strawberries, chopped banana, pineapple chunks, chopped cucumber, and lemon juice.
  - Add optional honey or agave syrup if needed.
  - Blend until smooth.

- **Serving Suggestions**
  - Garnish with a few whole strawberries or a slice of lemon for a vibrant touch.
  - Serve with a side of Greek yogurt or a sprinkle of granola for added protein and texture.

Calories: 120 kcal. Protein: 1.5g. Carbohydrates: 29g. Fat: 1g. Fiber: 4g

Lettuce Lemon Green Smoothie

Ingredients

 +  +

1 cup fresh lettuce (Romaine, Butterhead, etc)   1/2 green apple   1 tspn fresh ginger

 +

1/4 cucumber   1/2 lemon

+ 1/2 cup water or coconut water (and ice for a thicker smoothie)

Directions

- **Prepare Ingredients**
  - Wash the lettuce and cucumber thoroughly.
  - Core and chop the green apple.
  - Juice the lemon.
  - Grate the fresh ginger.

- **Blend Ingredients**
  - Start by adding the water or coconut water to the blender.
  - Add the lettuce, cucumber, green apple, lemon juice, and ginger.
  - Add optional honey or agave syrup if needed.
  - Blend until smooth.

- **Serving Suggestions**
  - For an extra touch, garnish with a slice of lemon or a cucumber wheel on the rim of the glass.

Calories: 90 kcal. Protein: 2g. Carbohydrates: 20g. Fat: 1g. Fiber: 6g

Zucchini Green Delight Smoothie

Calories: 180 kcal. Protein: 5g. Carbohydrates: 30g. Fat: 7g. Fiber: 8g

Ingredients

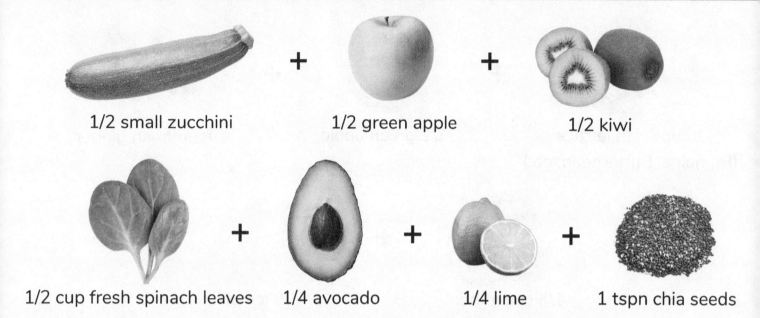

1/2 small zucchini + 1/2 green apple + 1/2 kiwi

1/2 cup fresh spinach leaves + 1/4 avocado + 1/4 lime + 1 tspn chia seeds

+ 1/2 cup water or coconut water (and ice for a thicker smoothie)

Directions

- **Prepare Ingredients**
  - Wash and chop the zucchini, green apple, kiwi, and spinach leaves.
  - Peel and pit the avocado.
  - Juice the lime.

- **Blend Ingredients**
  - In a blender, combine the chopped zucchini, green apple, kiwi, spinach leaves, avocado, coconut water, lime juice, and chia seeds.
  - Add the optional honey or maple syrup if desired.
  - Blend until smooth.

- **Serving Suggestions**
  - Garnish with a slice of kiwi or a sprinkle of chia seeds for a decorative touch.

Calories: 180 kcal. Protein: 5g. Carbohydrates: 30g. Fat: 7g. Fiber: 8g

CHAPTER 3: WEIGHT LOSS SMOOTHIES

Weight loss smoothies are an effective and enjoyable way to support your journey towards a healthier, leaner body. These nutrient-rich blends can help you manage your calorie intake while providing essential nutrients, promoting satiety, and boosting metabolism.

HOW SMOOTHIES CAN AID IN WEIGHT LOSS

1 Controlled Calorie Intake

Weight loss smoothies can help you manage your calorie intake by providing a controlled, portioned meal or snack option. By using ingredients that are low in calories but high in nutrients, you can create satisfying smoothies that keep you full without exceeding your daily calorie goals.

2 Nutrient Density

These smoothies are packed with nutrient-dense ingredients like fruits, vegetables, and superfoods, ensuring you get the vitamins, minerals, and antioxidants your body needs without extra calories. This helps support overall health and well-being, which is crucial for sustainable weight loss.

3 High Fiber Content

Weight loss smoothies include high-fiber ingredients such as leafy greens, fruits, seeds, and oats. Fiber helps promote satiety, reducing hunger and preventing overeating. It also aids digestion and helps maintain stable blood sugar levels, which is essential for weight management.

4 Hydration

Staying hydrated is essential for weight loss, as it helps control hunger, aids digestion, and supports overall metabolism. Many weight loss smoothies include hydrating ingredients like coconut water, water-rich fruits, and leafy greens, helping you meet your daily hydration needs.

5 Healthy Fats

Incorporating healthy fats from sources like avocados, nuts, seeds, and coconut oil can help increase satiety and provide essential fatty acids that support overall health. Healthy fats also help in the absorption of fat-soluble vitamins and can prevent cravings for unhealthy, high-calorie snacks.

6 Reduced Cravings

Weight loss smoothies can help curb cravings by providing a sweet and satisfying treat made from natural, wholesome ingredients. This can reduce the temptation to reach for sugary or processed foods, aiding in your weight loss efforts.

Fat-Burning Berry Blast Smoothie

Ingredients

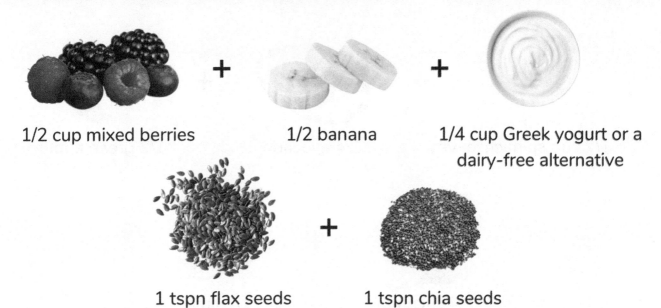

1/2 cup mixed berries + 1/2 banana + 1/4 cup Greek yogurt or a dairy-free alternative

1 tspn flax seeds + 1 tspn chia seeds

+ 1/2 cup unsweetened almond milk or another milk of choice

Directions

- **Prepare Ingredients**
  - Peel and chop the banana.
  - Measure out the mixed berries.

- **Blend Ingredients**
  - In a blender, combine the mixed berries, chopped banana, Greek yogurt, chia seeds, flax seeds, and almond milk.
  - Add the optional honey or maple syrup for sweetness.
  - Blend until smooth.

- **Serving Suggestions**
  - Garnish with a few whole berries or a sprinkle of chia seeds for a decorative touch.
  - Serve with a side of whole grain toast or a handful of nuts for a balanced snack.

Slimming Green Machine Smoothie

Ingredients

1/2 cup spinach leaves + 1/4 avocado + 1/2 green apple

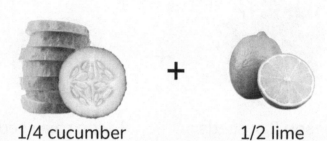

1/4 cucumber + 1/2 lime

+ 1 cup unsweetened almond milk or another milk of choice

Directions

- **Prepare Ingredients**
  - Peel and pit the avocado.
  - Core and chop the green apple.
  - Peel and chop the cucumber.
  - Juice the lime.

- **Blend Ingredients**
  - In a blender, combine the almond milk, spinach leaves, avocado, chopped green apple, chopped cucumber, lime juice, and optional honey or maple syrup.
  - Blend until smooth.

- **Serving Suggestions**
  - Garnish with a slice of lime or a few spinach leaves for a fresh presentation.
  - Serve with a side of whole-grain crackers or a handful of nuts for added protein and texture.

Calories: 180 kcal. Protein: 4g. Carbohydrates: 22g. Fat: 8g. Fiber: 7g

Metabolism Booster Smoothie

Ingredients

 +  +  +

| 1/2 cup spinach leaves | 1/4 cup pineapple chunks (fresh or frozen) | 1/2 green apple | 1/2 lemon |

 +  +  +

1/4 cucumber   1 tspn flax seeds   1 tspn chia seeds   1 tspn fresh ginger

+ 1/2 cup coconut water or unsweetened almond milk (and ice for a thicker smoothie)

Directions

- **Prepare Ingredients**
  - Core and chop the green apple.
  - Peel and chop the cucumber.
  - Peel and grate the fresh ginger.
  - Juice the lemon.

- **Blend Ingredients**
  - In a blender, combine the coconut water or unsweetened almond milk, spinach leaves, chopped green apple, chopped cucumber, pineapple chunks, grated ginger, lemon juice, chia seeds, and flax seeds.
  - Blend until smooth.

- **Serving Suggestions**
  - Garnish with a slice of lemon or a sprinkle of chia seeds for a vibrant presentation.
  - Serve with a side of whole grain toast or a handful of nuts for a balanced snack.

Calories: 160 kcal. Protein: 5g. Carbohydrates: 28g. Fat: 4g. Fiber: 8g

Tropical Weight Loss Wonder Smoothie

Ingredients

 +  +

1/4 cup mango chunks (fresh or frozen)   1/4 cup pineapple chunks (fresh or frozen)   1/2 lime

 +  +  +

1/2 banana   1 tspn flax seeds   1 tspn chia seeds   1/4 avocado

+ 1/2 cup coconut water or unsweetened almond milk (and ice for a thicker smoothie)

Directions

- **Prepare Ingredients**
  - Peel and chop the banana.
  - Peel and pit the avocado.
  - Juice the lime.

- **Blend Ingredients**
  - In a blender, combine the coconut water or almond milk, pineapple chunks, mango chunks, chopped banana, avocado, chia seeds, flax seeds, and lime juice.
  - Blend until smooth.

- **Serving Suggestions**
  - Garnish with a slice of lime or a few pineapple chunks for a tropical touch.
  - Serve with a side of Greek yogurt or a sprinkle of granola for added protein and texture.

Calories: 220 kcal. Protein: 5g. Carbohydrates: 35g. Fat: 9g. Fiber: 9g

Pineapple Protein Power Smoothie

Ingredients

 +  +

| 1/4 cup Greek yogurt or a dairy-free alternative | 1/4 cup pineapple chunks (fresh or frozen) | 1/2 scoop vanilla protein powder |

 +  +

| 1/2 banana | 1 tspn flax seeds | 1 tspn chia seeds |

+ 1/2 cup coconut water or unsweetened almond milk (and ice for a thicker smoothie)

Directions

- **Prepare Ingredients**
  - Peel and chop the banana.
  - Measure out the pineapple chunks.

- **Blend Ingredients**
  - In a blender, combine the coconut water or almond milk pineapple chunks, chopped banana, Greek yogurt, vanilla protein powder, chia seeds, and flax seeds.
  - Blend until smooth.
  - You can also add ice cubes for a chilled smoothie.

- **Serving Suggestions**
  - Garnish with a pineapple slice or a sprinkle of chia seeds for a decorative touch.
  - Serve with a side of whole grain toast or a handful of nuts for a balanced snack.

Citrus Weight Loss Shake

Ingredients

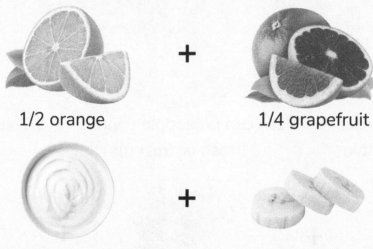

1/2 orange + 1/4 grapefruit

1/4 cup Greek yogurt or a dairy-free alternative + 1/2 banana

+ 1/2 cup coconut water or unsweetened almond milk (and ice for a thicker smoothie)

Directions

- **Prepare Ingredients**
  - Peel and segment the orange and grapefruit.
  - Peel the banana.

- **Blend Ingredients**
  - In a blender, combine the coconut water or almond milk, orange segments, grapefruit segments, banana, Greek yogurt, and optional honey or maple syrup.
  - Blend until smooth.

- **Serving Suggestions**
  - Garnish with a slice of orange or a sprinkle of chia seeds for a decorative touch.
  - Serve with a side of whole grain toast or a handful of nuts for a balanced snack.

Calories: 180 kcal. Protein: 6g. Carbohydrates: 35g. Fat: 2g. Fiber: 7g

Apple Cinnamon Fat Burner Smoothie

Ingredients

1/2 apple + 1/4 tspn cinnamon + 1/8 tspn ground ginger

1/2 tspn maca powder + 1 tspn almond butter + 1 tspn chia seeds

+ 1/2 cup unsweetened almond milk (and ice for a thicker smoothie)

Directions

- **Prepare Ingredients**
  - Core and chop the apple.
  - Grate the fresh ginger.

- **Blend Ingredients**
  - In a blender, combine the almond milk, chopped apple, ground cinnamon, ground ginger, chia seeds, maca powder and almond butter.
  - Blend until smooth.

- **Serving Suggestions**
  - Garnish with a sprinkle of cinnamon or a slice of apple for a festive touch.
  - Serve with a side of whole grain toast or a handful of nuts for a balanced snack.

Spinach Mango Delight Smoothie

Ingredients

 +

1/4 cup Greek yogurt or a dairy-free alternative

1/2 cup mango (fresh or frozen)

 +

1/2 cup spinach leaves

1/2 banana

+ 1/2 cup coconut water or unsweetened almond milk (and ice for a thicker smoothie)

Directions

- **Prepare Ingredients**
  - Measure out the spinach leaves.
  - Chop the mango.

- **Blend Ingredients**
  - In a blender, combine the coconut water or almond milk, spinach leaves, chopped mango, banana, Greek yogurt, and optional honey or maple syrup.
  - Blend until smooth.

- **Serving Suggestions**
  - Garnish with a slice of mango or a sprinkle of chia seeds for a decorative touch.
  - Serve with a side of whole grain crackers or a handful of nuts for added protein and texture.

Calories: 200 kcal. Protein: 5g. Carbohydrates: 40g. Fat: 3g. Fiber: 6g

Cucumber Mint Slimmer Smoothie

Ingredients

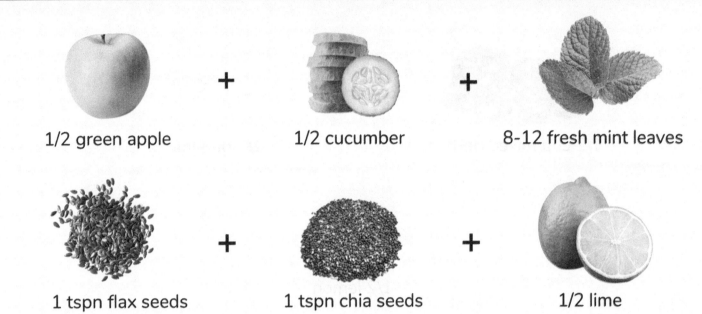

1/2 green apple   +   1/2 cucumber   +   8-12 fresh mint leaves

1 tspn flax seeds   +   1 tspn chia seeds   +   1/2 lime

+ 1/2 cup coconut water or unsweetened almond milk (and ice for a thicker smoothie)

Directions

- **Prepare Ingredients**
  - Peel and chop the cucumber.
  - Core and chop the green apple.
  - Juice the lime.

- **Blend Ingredients**
  - In a blender, combine the coconut water or almond milk, chopped cucumber, mint leaves, chopped green apple, lime juice, chia seeds, flax seeds, and optional honey or maple syrup.
  - Blend until smooth.

- **Serving Suggestions**
  - Garnish with a sprig of fresh mint or a slice of cucumber for a refreshing touch.
  - Serve with a side of whole grain toast or a handful of nuts for added protein and texture.

Calories: 200 kcal. Protein: 3g. Carbohydrates: 35g. Fat: 10g. Fiber: 7g

Lemon Berry Slim Down Smoothie

1/2 cup mixed berries

+

1/2 banana

1/2 lemon

+ 1 cup unsweetened almond milk (and ice for a thicker smoothie)

Directions

- **Prepare Ingredients**
  - Measure out the mixed berries.
  - Juice the lemon.
  - Peel and chop the banana.

- **Blend Ingredients**
  - In a blender, combine the almond milk, mixed berries, lemon juice, banana, and optional honey or maple syrup.
  - Blend until smooth.

- **Serving Suggestions**
  - Garnish with a few whole berries or a slice of lemon for a decorative touch.
  - Serve with a side of whole grain crackers or a handful of nuts for added protein and texture.

Calories: 150 kcal. Protein: 3g. Carbohydrates: 30g. Fat: 2g. Fiber: 6g

Watermelon Fat Melter Smoothie

Ingredients

 +  +

1 cup diced watermelon   1/4 cup strawberries   4-5 fresh mint leaves

 +

1/4 cup cucumber   1/2 lemon

+ 1/2 cup coconut water or unsweetened almond milk (and ice for a thicker smoothie)

Directions

- **Prepare Ingredients**
  - Dice the watermelon.
  - Hull the strawberries.
  - Peel and chop the cucumber.
  - Juice the lemon.

- **Blend Ingredients**
  - In a blender, combine the coconut water or almond milk, diced watermelon, strawberries, chopped cucumber, fresh mint leaves, lemon juice, and optional honey or maple syrup.
  - Blend until smooth.

- **Serving Suggestions**
  - Garnish with a sprig of mint or a slice of watermelon for a refreshing touch.
  - Serve with a side of whole grain crackers or a handful of nuts for added protein and texture.

Kiwi Coconut Slimmer Smoothie

Ingredients

1 kiwi   +   1/4 banana

1/2 cup coconut milk   +   1/4 tspn spirulina powder

+ 1/4 cup coconut water (and ice for a thicker smoothie)

Directions

- **Prepare Ingredients**
  - Peel and chop the kiwi.
  - Peel the banana.

- **Blend Ingredients**
  - In a blender, combine the coconut milk, coconut water, chopped kiwis, banana, spirulina powder, and optional honey or maple syrup.
  - Blend until smooth.

- **Serving Suggestions**
  - Garnish with a slice of kiwi or a sprinkle of coconut flakes for a tropical touch.
  - Serve with a side of whole grain toast or a handful of nuts for added protein and texture.

Calories: 200 kcal. Protein: 2g. Carbohydrates: 30g. Fat: 10g. Fiber: 5g

Strawberry Lemonade Slimmer Smoothie

Ingredients

1/2 cup strawberries

1 lemon

1/4 cup Greek yogurt or
a dairy-free alternative

+ 1/2 cup water (and ice for a thicker smoothie)

Directions

- **Prepare Ingredients**
  - Hull the strawberries.
  - Juice the lemon.

- **Blend Ingredients**
  - In a blender, combine the Greek yogurt or alternative, water, strawberries, lemon juice, and optional honey or maple syrup.
  - Blend until smooth.

- **Serving Suggestions**
  - Garnish with a slice of lemon or a strawberry for a decorative touch.
  - Serve with a side of whole grain crackers or a handful of nuts for added protein and texture.

Ginger Peach Fat Burner Smoothie

Ingredients

 +  +

1 peach   1 tspn fresh ginger   1/4 tspn ground cinnamon

 +

1/4 tspn cayenne pepper (optional)   1/4 cup Greek yogurt or a dairy-free alternative

+ 1/2 cup water (and ice for a thicker smoothie)

Directions

- **Prepare Ingredients**
  - Pit and chop the peach.
  - Grate the fresh ginger.

- **Blend Ingredients**
  - In a blender, combine the Greek yogurt or alternative, water, chopped peaches, grated ginger, ground cinnamon, cayenne pepper, and optional honey or maple syrup.
  - Blend until smooth.

- **Serving Suggestions**
  - Garnish with a sprinkle of ground cinnamon or a slice of peach for a decorative touch.
  - Serve with a side of whole grain crackers or a handful of nuts for added protein and texture.

Calories: 120 kcal. Protein: 4g. Carbohydrates: 25g. Fat: 1g. Fiber: 4g

Turmeric Pineapple Slimmer Smoothie

Ingredients

 +

1/2 cup diced pineapple   1/2 banana

 +

1/4 cup coconut milk   1/4 tspn ground turmeric

+ 1/4 cup water (and ice for a thicker smoothie)

Directions

- **Prepare Ingredients**
  - Dice the pineapple.
  - Peel and chop the banana.

- **Blend Ingredients**
  - In a blender, combine the coconut milk, water, diced pineapple, banana, ground turmeric, and optional honey or maple syrup.
  - Blend until smooth.

- **Serving Suggestions**
  - Garnish with a sprinkle of ground turmeric or a slice of pineapple for a tropical touch.
  - Serve with a side of whole grain crackers or a handful of nuts for added protein and texture.

Raspberry Detox Slimmer Smoothie

Ingredients

 +

1/2 cup raspberries   1/4 cup blueberries

 +  +

1/4 cucumber   4-6 fresh mint leaves   1/2 lemon

+ 1/2 cup water (and ice for a thicker smoothie)

Directions

- **Prepare Ingredients**
  - Measure out the raspberries and blueberries.
  - Peel and chop the cucumber.
  - Juice the lemon.

- **Blend Ingredients**
  - In a blender, combine the water, raspberries, blueberries, chopped cucumber, fresh mint leaves, lemon juice, and optional honey or maple syrup.
  - Blend until smooth.

- **Serving Suggestions**
  - Garnish with a few extra raspberries or a sprig of mint for a decorative touch.
  - Serve with a side of whole grain toast or a handful of nuts for added protein and texture.

Calories: 100 kcal. Protein: 2g. Carbohydrates: 25g. Fat: 1g. Fiber: 6g

Blueberry Almond Slimmer Smoothie

Ingredients

 +  +

1/2 cup blueberries   1/2 banana   1 tspn chia seeds

 +  +

1/8 cup almonds   1 tspn almond butter   1/4 tspn vanilla extract

+ 1/2 cup almond milk (and ice for a thicker smoothie)

Directions

- **Prepare Ingredients**
  - Measure out and wash the blueberries.
  - Peel the banana.
  - Soak and peel the almonds.

- **Blend Ingredients**
  - In a blender, combine the almond milk, blueberries, banana, soaked and peeled almonds, almond butter, chia seeds, optional honey or maple syrup, and vanilla extract.
  - Blend until smooth.

- **Serving Suggestions**
  - Garnish with a sprinkle of cinnamon or a few whole blueberries for a decorative touch.
  - Serve with a side of whole grain toast or a handful of nuts for added protein and texture.

Papaya Protein Slimmer Smoothie

Ingredients

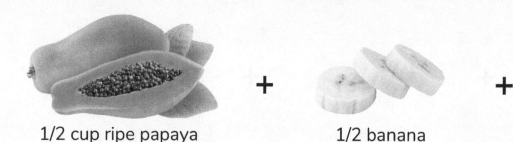 +

1/2 cup ripe papaya   +   1/2 banana   +   1/4 tspn flax seeds

   +

1/4 cup Greek yogurt or a dairy-free alternative   +   1/2 scoop vanilla protein powder

+   1/4 cup almond milk or other preferred milk (and ice for a thicker smoothie)

Directions

- **Prepare Ingredients**
  - Peel and dice the papaya.
  - Peel the banana.

- **Blend Ingredients**
  - In a blender, combine the almond milk, diced papaya, banana, Greek yogurt, vanilla protein powder, optional honey or maple syrup, and ground flax seeds.
  - Blend until smooth.

- **Serving Suggestions**
  - Garnish with a few papaya slices or a sprinkle of flax seeds for a decorative touch.
  - Serve with a side of whole grain toast or a handful of nuts for added protein and texture.

Calories: 220 kcal. Protein: 15g. Carbohydrates: 35g. Fat: 4g. Fiber: 5g

CHAPTER 4: ENERGY-BOOSTING SMOOTHIES

Energy-boosting smoothies are a fantastic way to fuel your body with the nutrients it needs to maintain high energy levels throughout the day. An ideal choice for busy mornings, post-workout recovery, or anytime you need an extra pick-me-up.

THE ROLE OF SMOOTHIES IN INCREASING ENERGY LEVELS

1 **Nutrient Density**

Energy-boosting smoothies are packed with nutrient-dense ingredients, including fruits, vegetables, nuts, seeds, and superfoods. These components supply your body with essential vitamins, minerals, and antioxidants that play crucial roles in energy production and overall health.

2 **Balanced Macronutrients**

A well-balanced energy smoothie includes a mix of macronutrients: carbohydrates, proteins, and healthy fats. Carbohydrates from fruits and whole grains provide quick energy, proteins from sources like Greek yogurt or protein powders help sustain energy levels and repair muscles, and healthy fats from nuts and seeds offer long-lasting energy and support brain function.

3 **Natural Sugars**

Unlike processed snacks and sugary drinks that cause energy spikes and crashes, smoothies contain natural sugars from fruits that are paired with fiber, slowing down sugar absorption and providing a steady energy release. This helps maintain consistent energy levels without the crash.

4 **Hydration**

Many energy-boosting smoothies are made with hydrating ingredients like coconut water, water-rich fruits, and leafy greens. Proper hydration is essential for maintaining energy levels, as even mild dehydration can lead to fatigue and decreased cognitive function.

5 **Antioxidants**

Ingredients like berries, dark leafy greens, and nuts are rich in antioxidants, which combat oxidative stress and inflammation in the body. By reducing these factors, antioxidants help improve cellular energy production and overall vitality.

(6) Adaptogens and Superfoods

Many energy-boosting smoothies incorporate adaptogens and superfoods like maca powder, spirulina, and chia seeds. Adaptogens help the body manage stress and maintain balance, while superfoods provide concentrated doses of essential nutrients that support energy and well-being.

(7) Sustained Energy Release

The combination of fiber, protein, and healthy fats in energy-boosting smoothies ensures a sustained release of energy. Fiber from fruits and vegetables slows digestion, preventing rapid blood sugar spikes and providing a more gradual energy boost.

(8) Easy Digestion

Smoothies are easy to digest, making them a great option for a quick energy boost without feeling weighed down. The blending process breaks down the fiber and cell walls of fruits and vegetables, making the nutrients more readily available for absorption.

Powerhouse Protein Smoothie

Ingredients

 +  +

1/2 cup spinach leaves   1/2 banana   1/2 tspn chia seeds

 +  +

1/4 cup Greek yogurt or a dairy-free alternative   1/2 scoop chocolate or vanilla protein powder   1 tspn peanut or almond butter

+ 1/2 cup unsweetened almond milk (and ice for a thicker smoothie)

Directions

- **Prepare Ingredients**
  - Rinse the spinach leaves
  - Peel and chop the banana.

- **Blend Ingredients**
  - In a blender, combine the spinach leaves, banana, Greek yogurt, protein powder, peanut butter, optional honey or maple syrup, chia seeds, and almond milk.
  - Blend until smooth.

- **Serving Suggestions**
  - Garnish with a sprinkle of chia seeds or a few spinach leaves for a decorative touch.
  - Serve with a side of whole grain toast or a handful of nuts for added protein and texture.

Calories: 300 kcal. Protein: 25g. Carbohydrates: 35g. Fat: 10g. Fiber: 6g

Energizing Green Power Smoothie

Ingredients

 +  +  +

1/2 cup spinach leaves   1/2 banana   1/2 tspn chia seeds   1/4 cup kale leaves (stems removed)

+ +

1/4 cup Greek yogurt or a dairy-free alternative   1/4 avocado   1/2 teaspoon spirulina powder

+ 1/2 cup unsweetened almond milk (and ice for a thicker smoothie)

Directions

- **Prepare Ingredients**
  - Rinse the spinach and kale leaves
  - Peel the banana.
  - Scoop out the avocado.

- **Blend Ingredients**
  - In a blender, combine the spinach leaves, kale leaves, banana, avocado, Greek yogurt, optional honey or maple syrup, spirulina powder, chia seeds, and coconut water.
  - Blend until smooth.

- **Serving Suggestions**
  - Garnish with a sprinkle of chia seeds or a few kale or spinach leaves for a decorative touch.
  - Serve with a side of whole grain toast or a handful of nuts for added protein and texture.

Nutty Banana Boost Smoothie

Ingredients

1 banana   +   1 tspn chia seeds

1/4 cup Greek yogurt or a dairy-free alternative   +   1/4 tspn ground cinnamon   +   1 tspn peanut or almond butter

+ 1/2 cup unsweetened almond milk (and ice for a thicker smoothie)

Directions

- **Prepare Ingredients**
  - Peel the banana.

- **Blend Ingredients**
  - In a blender, combine the bananas, Greek yogurt, almond butter, optional honey or maple syrup, chia seeds, almond milk, and cinnamon.
  - Blend until smooth.

- **Serving Suggestions**
  - Garnish with a sprinkle of chia seeds or a dash of cinnamon for a decorative touch.
  - Serve with a side of whole grain toast or a handful of nuts for added protein and texture.

Calories: 300 kcal. Protein: 10g. Carbohydrates: 45g. Fat: 12g. Fiber: 6g

Tropical Energy Blast Smoothie

Ingredients

 +  +

| 1/2 mango | 1/2 cup pineapple chunks (fresh or frozen) | 1/4 cup orange juice (freshly squeezed preferred) |

 +  +

| 1/4 cup Greek yogurt or a dairy-free alternative | 1/2 banana | 1/2 tspn chia seeds |

+ 1/2 cup coconut water or water (and ice for a thicker smoothie)

Directions

- **Prepare Ingredients**
  - Peel and chop the mango and banana.
  - Measure out the pineapple chunks.
  - Squeeze orange juice.

- **Blend Ingredients**
  - In a blender, combine the pineapple chunks, mango, banana, Greek yogurt, orange juice, optional honey or maple syrup, chia seeds, and coconut water.
  - Blend until smooth.

- **Serving Suggestions**
  - Garnish with a sprinkle of shredded coconut or chia seeds for a decorative touch.
  - Serve with a side of tropical fruit salad or a handful of nuts for added protein and texture.

Citrus Energy Elixir Smoothie

Ingredients

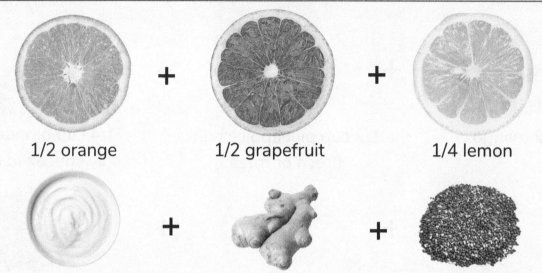

1/2 orange + 1/2 grapefruit + 1/4 lemon

1/4 cup Greek yogurt or a dairy-free alternative + 1 tspn grated ginger + 1/2 tspn chia seeds

+ 1/4 cup coconut water or other preferred liquid base (and ice for a thicker smoothie)

Directions

- **Prepare Ingredients**
  - Peel and segment the orange and grapefruit.
  - Juice the lemon.

- **Blend Ingredients**
  - In a blender, combine the orange segments, grapefruit segments, lemon juice, Greek yogurt, coconut water, optional honey or maple syrup, chia seeds, and grated ginger.
  - Blend until smooth.

- **Serving Suggestions**
  - Garnish with a sprinkle of chia seeds or a slice of citrus fruit for a decorative touch.
  - Serve with a side of nuts or seeds for added protein and texture.

Calories: 220 kcal. Protein: 8g. Carbohydrates: 40g. Fat: 4g. Fiber: 6g

Berry Protein Punch Smoothie

Ingredients

 +  +

| 1/2 cup mixed berries | 1/2 banana | 1/2 scoop vanilla protein powder |

 +  +

1/4 cup Greek yogurt or a dairy-free alternative — 1/2 tspn hemp seeds — 1/2 tspn chia seeds

+ 1/2 cup unsweetened almond milk (and ice for a thicker smoothie)

Directions

- **Prepare Ingredients**
  - Peel and chop the banana.
  - Measure out and wash the berries.

- **Blend Ingredients**
  - In a blender, combine the mixed berries, banana, protein powder, almond milk, Greek yogurt, optional honey or maple syrup, chia seeds, and hemp seeds.
  - Blend until smooth.

- **Serving Suggestions**
  - Garnish with a few whole berries or a sprinkle of chia seeds for a decorative touch.
  - Serve with a handful of nuts or a piece of whole-grain toast for added protein and texture.

Matcha Green Energy Smoothie

Ingredients

 **+**  **+**

| 1/2 tspn matcha powder | 1/4 cup Greek yogurt or a dairy-free alternative | 1/4 tspn spirulina powder |

 **+**  **+**  **+**

1/4 cucumber   1/4 avocado   1/2 cup spinach leaves   1/2 banana

+ 1/4 cup coconut water or other preferred liquid base (and ice for a thicker smoothie)

Directions

- **Prepare Ingredients**
  - Peel and chop the banana, avocado, and cucumber.

- **Blend Ingredients**
  - In a blender, combine the matcha powder, spirulina powder, banana, avocado, spinach leaves, cucumber, optional honey or maple syrup, coconut water, and Greek yogurt.
  - Blend until smooth.

- **Serving Suggestions**
  - Garnish with a sprinkle of matcha powder or a slice of cucumber for a decorative touch.
  - Serve with a side of nuts or seeds for added protein and texture.

Calories: 250 kcal. Protein: 8g. Carbohydrates: 35g. Fat: 10g. Fiber: 8g

Mango Chia Energy Smoothie

Ingredients

1/2 mango

+

1/4 cup Greek yogurt or
a dairy-free alternative

1/2 banana

+

1 tspn chia seeds

+ 1/4 cup coconut water or other preferred liquid base (and ice for a thicker smoothie)

Directions

- **Prepare Ingredients**
  - Peel and dice the mango and banana.

- **Blend Ingredients**
  - In a blender, combine the diced mango, banana, chia seeds, coconut water, Greek yogurt, and optional honey or maple syrup.
  - Blend until smooth.

- **Serving Suggestions**
  - Garnish with a sprinkle of chia seeds or a slice of mango for a decorative touch.
  - Serve with a side of nuts or seeds for added protein and texture.

Pineapple Protein Surge Smoothie

Ingredients

 +

1/2 cup pineapple chunks (fresh or frozen)

1/2 scoop vanilla protein powder

 +  +

1/4 cup Greek yogurt or a dairy-free alternative

1/2 banana

1 tspn chia seeds

+ 1/4 cup coconut water or other preferred liquid base (and ice for a thicker smoothie)

Directions

- **Prepare Ingredients**
  - Peel and chop the pineapple and banana.

- **Blend Ingredients**
  - In a blender, combine the pineapple chunks, banana, Greek yogurt, coconut water, protein powder, chia seeds, and optional honey or maple syrup.
  - Blend until smooth.

- **Serving Suggestions**
  - Garnish with a pineapple wedge or a sprinkle of chia seeds for a decorative touch.
  - Serve with a side of nuts or seeds for added protein and texture.

Calories: 250 kcal. Protein: 20g. Carbohydrates: 40g. Fat: 3g. Fiber: 6g

Kale Banana Energy Smoothie

Ingredients

1/4 cup kale leaves
(stems removed)

+

1 tspn peanut or
almond butter

1/4 cup Greek yogurt or
a dairy-free alternative

+

1/2 banana

+ 1/4 cup coconut water or other preferred liquid base (and ice for a thicker smoothie)

Directions

- **Prepare Ingredients**
  - Remove the stems from the kale leaves.
  - Peel the banana.

- **Blend Ingredients**
  - In a blender, combine the kale leaves, banana, coconut water, Greek yogurt, almond butter, and optional honey or maple syrup.
  - Blend until smooth.

- **Serving Suggestions**
  - Garnish with a kale leaf or a sprinkle of chia seeds for a decorative touch.
  - Serve with a side of nuts or seeds for added protein and texture.

Chocolate Coffee Energizer Smoothie

Ingredients

 **+**

1/4 cup cold brew coffee

1 tspn peanut or almond butter

 **+**

1 tspn cocoa powder

1/2 banana

+ 1/4 cup almond milk or other preferred liquid base (and ice for a thicker smoothie)

Directions

- **Prepare Ingredients**
  - Peel and chop the banana.

- **Blend Ingredients**
  - In a blender, combine the banana, cold brew coffee, almond milk, cocoa powder, almond butter, and optional honey or maple syrup.
  - Blend until smooth.

- **Serving Suggestions**
  - Garnish with a sprinkle of cocoa powder or a drizzle of honey for a decorative touch.
  - Serve with a side of nuts or seeds for added protein and texture.

Calories: 200 kcal. Protein: 5g. Carbohydrates: 30g. Fat: 8g. Fiber: 6g

Kiwi Energy Zest Smoothie

Ingredients

1 kiwi   +   1/4 banana

1/4 cup Greek yogurt or
a dairy-free alternative   +   1/2 cup spinach leaves

+ 1/4 cup coconut water or other preferred liquid base (and ice for a thicker smoothie)

Directions

- **Prepare Ingredients**
  - Peel and dice the kiwi.
  - Peel and chop the banana.

- **Blend Ingredients**
  - In a blender, combine the diced kiwis, banana, spinach leaves, coconut water, Greek yogurt, and optional honey or maple syrup.
  - Blend until smooth.

- **Serving Suggestions**
  - Garnish with a slice of kiwi or a sprinkle of chia seeds for a decorative touch.
  - Serve with a side of nuts or seeds for added protein and texture.

Papaya Protein Boost Smoothie

Ingredients

1/2 cup ripe papaya

1/2 banana

1/4 cup Greek yogurt or
a dairy-free alternative

1 tspn almond
butter

+ 1/4 cup almond milk or other preferred liquid base (and ice for a thicker smoothie)

Directions

- **Prepare Ingredients**
  - If using fresh papaya, peel, seed, and dice it.
  - Peel and chop the banana.

- **Blend Ingredients**
  - In a blender, combine the diced papaya, banana, Greek yogurt, almond milk, almond butter, and optional honey or maple syrup.
  - Blend until smooth.

- **Serving Suggestions**
  - Garnish with a slice of papaya or a sprinkle of chia seeds for a decorative touch.
  - Serve with a side of nuts or seeds for added protein and texture.

Calories: 200 kcal. Protein: 8g. Carbohydrates: 30g. Fat: 8g. Fiber: 6g

Apple Cinnamon Energy Smoothie

Ingredients

1/2 apple + 1/2 banana

1/4 cup Greek yogurt or a dairy-free alternative + 1/4 tspn ground cinnamon + 1 tspn peanut or almond butter

+ 1/4 cup almond milk or other preferred liquid base (and ice for a thicker smoothie)

Directions

- **Prepare Ingredients**
  - Core and chop the apple, keeping the skin on for added fiber.
  - Peel and chop the banana.

- **Blend Ingredients**
  - In a blender, combine the chopped apple, banana, Greek yogurt, almond milk, almond butter, ground cinnamon, and optional honey or maple syrup.
  - Blend until smooth.

- **Serving Suggestions**
  - Garnish with a sprinkle of ground cinnamon or a few apple slices for a decorative touch.
  - Serve with a side of nuts or seeds for added protein and texture.

CHAPTER 5: SMOOTHIE TROUBLESHOOTING

Even the most experienced smoothie makers encounter issues from time to time. Here are some common problems and practical solutions to ensure your smoothies are always delicious and satisfying.

COMMON ISSUES AND SOLUTIONS

1 Too Thick?

Add more liquid (water, milk, or juice) a little at a time and blend again until you reach the desired consistency.

2 Too Thin?

Add more frozen fruits, ice, or a thickening agent like yogurt, avocado, or nut butter. Blend until smooth.

3 Bitter Taste?

Add a natural sweetener such as honey, maple syrup, or dates. Alternatively, add more fruits like banana or mango to balance the bitterness

4 Not Smooth Enough?

Ensure you are blending long enough and at the right speed. Start on a low speed and gradually increase to high. You may also need to add more liquid.

5 Separation?

Blend your smoothie again before drinking. Using ingredients like banana, avocado, or yogurt can help improve the texture and reduce separation.

6 Lack of Flavor?

Enhance the flavor by adding a pinch of salt, a splash of citrus juice, or a bit of your favorite spice like cinnamon or ginger.

7 Too Sweet?

Add a squeeze of lemon or lime juice to balance the sweetness. Alternatively, add more greens or a bit of plain yogurt.

FREQUENTLY ASKED QUESTIONS

HOW CAN I MAKE MY SMOOTHIE MORE FILLING?

Add protein sources like Greek yogurt, protein powder, nut butter, or chia seeds. Healthy fats from avocado, nuts, or seeds can also make a smoothie more satisfying.

CAN I PREPARE SMOOTHIES IN ADVANCE?

Yes, you can prepare smoothie packs by combining all the ingredients in a freezer-safe bag and storing them in the freezer. When ready, just add liquid and blend.

HOW DO I CLEAN MY BLENDER EFFECTIVELY?

Fill the blender halfway with warm water and a few drops of dish soap. Blend on high for 30 seconds, then rinse thoroughly.

WHAT ARE SOME GOOD LIQUID BASES FOR SMOOTHIES?

Water, dairy milk, almond milk, coconut milk, soy milk, and fruit juices are popular choices. Choose based on your dietary preferences and flavor profile.

HOW DO I INCORPORATE GREENS WITHOUT THE STRONG TASTE?

Start with mild-tasting greens like spinach or baby kale. Pair them with sweet fruits like banana, pineapple, or mango to mask the taste.

CAN I USE FROZEN FRUITS AND VEGETABLES?

Absolutely! Frozen produce is often more convenient and can help create a thicker, colder smoothie. It also retains much of its nutritional value.

HOW CAN I REDUCE THE SUGAR CONTENT IN MY SMOOTHIES?

Use more vegetables and less fruit, avoid adding sweeteners, and opt for unsweetened liquid bases. Ingredients like avocado, cucumber, and celery add volume without adding sugar.

CONCLUSION

Incorporating smoothies into your daily routine is a fantastic step. Remember, every smoothie you make is not just a drink but a commitment to your well-being. As you explore and enjoy the recipes in this book, know that you are nourishing your body and mind.

Your health journey is unique and personal. Keep experimenting with different ingredients, flavors, and combinations to find what works best for you. Celebrate each small victory and be kind to yourself on this path to better health.

Consistency is key, so make a habit of including nutritious smoothies in your diet, and let each blend be a reminder of your dedication to a healthier, happier you.

Tips for Ongoing Smoothie Experimentation and Enjoyment:

1. **Mix and Match.** Don't be afraid to swap out ingredients based on what you have available or what you enjoy the most. Every smoothie recipe can be a template for endless possibilities.
2. **Seasonal Freshness.** Use seasonal fruits and vegetables for the best flavor and nutritional value. This also keeps your smoothie routine exciting and varied.
3. **Superfood Boosts.** Experiment with different superfoods like chia seeds, spirulina, or maca root to enhance the health benefits of your smoothies.
4. **Taste and Texture.** Adjust the thickness and sweetness of your smoothies to suit your preferences. Add more liquid for a thinner consistency or a bit of honey or maple syrup for extra sweetness.
5. **Pre-prep for Convenience.** Prepare your ingredients in advance and store them in the freezer. This makes smoothie-making quick and easy, especially on busy mornings.

Thank you for joining me on this journey. Here's to a future filled with vibrant health, delicious smoothies, and endless enjoyment!

ENJOYED THE BOOK?

Your feedback means the world to me. If you found the smoothie recipes helpful and delicious, please take a moment to share your thoughts.

Simply scan the QR code to leave a review. Your insights help us improve and reach more smoothie lovers like you.

Thank you for your support!

DISCLAIMER

The information in this book is based on the author's research, experiences, and knowledge as of the publication date. It is intended for informational purposes only and should not be considered as medical advice. The author is not a licensed health professional, and readers should consult with a healthcare provider before making any significant changes to their diet or lifestyle, especially if they have any pre-existing medical conditions or are taking medications.

The author disclaims any liability arising directly or indirectly from the use of the information contained in this book. The recipes and nutritional information provided are estimates and may vary based on ingredient brands, quantities, and preparation methods. Individual results may vary.

Note: If you have allergies or dietary restrictions, please review all ingredients carefully to ensure they are safe for your consumption. Always prioritize your health and safety.

By using this book, you acknowledge that you have read, understood, and agreed to these terms and conditions.

COPYRIGHT

Contact Information:
Rosemary Moss
rosemary.m.books@gmail.com

Made in the USA
Las Vegas, NV
23 September 2024

95653892R10044